Fun Sushi

get started
making

Fun
Sushi

step-by-step recipes
for creative deco sushi

Little Miss Bento
Shirley Wong

 **Marshall Cavendish**
Cuisine

Shirley Wong, aka Little Miss Bento, became an online sensation and gained a huge following when she started posting her adorable Japanese bento lunchbox creations and unique deco sushi rolls on her blog and social media channels.

As the top bento artist and blogger in Singapore, Shirley has won many awards for her bento creations and is often featured on local and international media. She is currently the only Singaporean to be certified under the Japan Sushi Instructor Association in Tokyo, and she conducts bento classes and workshops to share her skills.

The recipes in this book were taken from *Kawaii Deco Sushi*. Shirley's first book, *Kawaii Bento* (2015), is a bestseller.

Follow Shirley online and share in her kawaii adventures:

Blog | littlemissbento.com
Facebook | www.facebook.com/littlemissbento
Instagram | Twitter | Snapchat | Pinterest | @littlemissbento
Email | littlemissbento@gmail.com

This book is for my mother
who laid the foundation
for my culinary adventures.

Contents

INTRODUCTION • 9

COOKING SUSHI RICE • 10

MEASURING COOKED SUSHI RICE • 12

SHAPING COOKED SUSHI RICE • 13

SPREADING SUSHI RICE • 14

SHAPING A TEARDROP-SHAPED ROLL • 15

SLICING SUSHI ROLLS • 16

SUSHI SEAWEED 101 • 17

MAKING A GRILLED OMELETTE (TAMAGOYAKI) • 20

BASIC FLOWER • 22

BEE • 26

SAKURA FLOWER • 30

CHESTNUT • 34

WATERMELON • 38

LEMON • 42

CANDY • 46

CHICK • 50

SAILING BOAT • 54

HEART • 58

WEIGHTS & MEASURES • 62

Introduction

Kazarimaki-sushi, translated as decorative sushi rolls or deco sushi, is a modern way of presenting sushi rolls in a highly creative way. It originated from the Boso Peninsula of Japan, where thick sushi rolls or futo-maki are common.

In this book, I'll show you how you can make your own deco sushi with the use and placement of various ingredients. And once you master the basics, you can start creating your own designs!

Deco sushi rolls are perfect for serving as finger food at parties, for bringing along to picnics, as well as for packing into bento boxes. What's more, these sushi rolls are not only tasty, they will delight, surprise and impress!

I have specially included detailed sections on basic techniques and step-by-step photographs with every recipe to guide you as you make these adorable sushi rolls.

Have fun making these kawaii (cute) deco sushi!

Little Miss Bento
Shirley Wong

Cooking Sushi Rice

Ingredients

1 cup Japanese rice

180 ml mineral water

1^1/$_2$ Tbsp rice vinegar

1 Tbsp castor sugar

^{1}/$_2$ tsp salt

Method

1. Rinse the rice about three times. Do not rub the rice grains, but use your hand to swirl the water gently. Drain.

2. Add the mineral water to the rice and let soak for at least 30 minutes.

3. Cook the rice in a rice cooker according to the manufacturer's instructions.

4. When the rice is done, let rest for 15–20 minutes in the rice cooker before transferring to a *hangiri* wooden rice tub.

5. Mix the vinegar, sugar and salt together.

6. Add the vinegar mixture to the rice and mix with a spatula, using a gentle slicing action to avoid mashing the rice grains.

7. If the rice is too wet, fan the rice as you mix.

8. Mix until the vinegar is absorbed by the rice. The rice grains will be shiny. Set aside and cover with a damp, lint-free cloth.

 TIP

If using Japonica hybrid rice, increase the amount of cooking liquid by 5–10% as the grains tend to be drier.

Normal drinking water can be used to cook the rice, but using mineral water will make the cooked rice more fluffy and have a beautiful gleam.

1 cup raw rice will yield approximately 300 g cooked rice.

Measuring Cooked Sushi Rice

To form the various parts of a design, you will need to portion out the rice as specified in the recipe. After weighing the rice in the required portions, cover with cling wrap to prevent the rice from drying out.

Shaping Cooked Sushi Rice

Many recipes call for the rice to be arranged in mountains (think of mountain ranges). To do this, shape the portion of rice into a triangular strip about 10-cm long. Form the number of rice mountains directed in the recipe.

Spreading Sushi Rice

To make spreading the rice easier, divide the portion of rice into a few parts and space them out on the sheet of seaweed. Use your fingers to press and spread the rice evenly on the seaweed. For the final sushi roll to be even, spread the rice evenly to the edges of the seaweed, leaving a gap at one or both ends to seal the sushi roll.

Shaping A Teardrop-Shaped Roll

When making a teardrop-shaped roll, use the sushi bamboo mat to squeeze one side of the roll so it is sharper on one side.

Slicing Sushi Rolls

It is best to use a specialised sushi knife to slice sushi rolls, but a sharp kitchen knife makes a good substitute.

When slicing sushi rolls, do not push the knife down on the roll. Instead, cut using a quick sawing motion parallel to your worktop.

The recipes in this book were designed to yield 4 slices. Slice the sushi roll down the centre in half, then halve each piece.

Clean the knife after each cut to ensure clean and neat slices.

Sushi Seaweed 101

Supermarkets stock two sizes of sushi seaweed—the full-size (20.5-cm x 19-cm) and the half-size (19-cm x 9.5-cm). In this book, I use the half-size sheet, and refer to it as 1 sheet. If the half-size sheets are not available, get the full-size sheets and cut them in half.

Full-size sheet

Half-size sheet
(1 sheet)

The recipes may also call for different sizes of sushi seaweed. The standard sizes required are $2/3$ sheet, $1/3$ sheet, $1/2$ sheet, $1/4$ sheet and $1/8$ sheet.

There are two sides to a sheet of sushi seaweed—the glossy side and the rough side. The glossy side should face outwards. Arrange the rice on the rough side.

Most of the recipes in this book require more than one sheet of sushi seaweed to enclose the design. This will be specified in the recipes. For example: 1 sheet + 1/3 sheet, joined. To join the sheets of sushi seaweed, stick them together by pressing a few grains of sushi rice on the edge of the sushi seaweed.

Some of the recipes in this book may require you to fold the sheet of sushi seaweed. To prevent the seaweed from breaking or tearing when folded, dab the folding line with a damp lint-free cloth.

When cutting seaweed, make a single cut through with a sharp knife. Do not drag the knife across the sheet as it would cause the seaweed to break. Alternatively, use a pair of scissors to cut the seaweed.

Making A Grilled Omelette
(Tamagoyaki)

~~~ Ingredients ~~~

2 eggs

2 Tbsp dashi stock

1 tsp Japanese white soy
  sauce (*shiro shoyu*)

1 tsp sugar

Cooking oil as needed

~~~ Method ~~~

1. Beat the eggs in a measuring cup to facilitate the pouring of
the egg later. Add the dashi stock, soy sauce and sugar and beat
well to mix.

2. Heat a little oil in a *tamagoyaki* pan.

3. Pour a quarter of the egg mixture into the pan. Tilt the pan so
the egg coats the base of the pan.

4. When the sides are cooked, roll the egg up from the other end
towards the handle of the pan. Push the egg roll to the other side
of the pan and pour in another quarter of the egg mixture. Repeat
to cook and roll until the egg mixture is used up.

Note

This recipe yields a small grilled
omelette. For a larger omelette,
adjust the portions.

Basic Flower

Ingredients

1 sheet + $^1/_3$ sheet of seaweed, joined

6 x $^1/_3$ sheet of seaweed

1 strip of seaweed, 10-cm x 1-cm

125 g white sushi rice, divided

125 g pink sushi rice (Mix evenly: 100 g white sushi rice + 25 g pink fish floss (*sakura denbu*)), divided into 5 parts, each 25 g

1 small cheese sausage, 10-cm long

5 spinach stalks, each 10-cm long, blanched

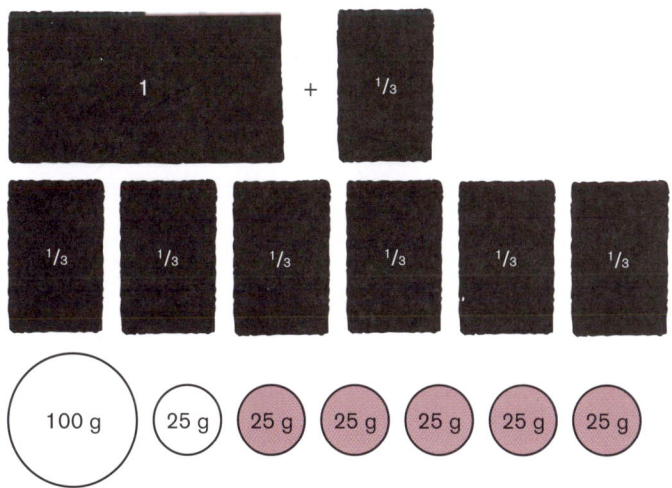

~~~~~~~~~~ Method ~~~~~~~~~~

1. Wrap the sausage with ¹/₃ sheet of seaweed for the centre of the flower. Set aside.

2. Shape each 25 g of pink rice into a 10-cm rod and wrap with ¹/₃ sheet of seaweed.

3. Arrange the rice rolls around the wrapped sausage and in the shape of a flower. Place a spinach stalk between each flower petal.

4. Wrap the flower roll with a thin strip of seaweed to keep it together. Set aside.

5. Spread 100 g white rice on the 1¹/₃ sheet of seaweed, leaving a 5-cm gap at one end.

6. Place the flower roll in the centre and start rolling up the roll.

7. Use the remaining white rice to fill any gaps before closing the roll.

8. Slice the roll into 4 pieces.

Bee

1 sheet + $^1/_3$ sheet of seaweed, joined

1 x $^2/_3$ sheet of seaweed

1 x $^1/_2$ sheet of seaweed

130 g white sushi rice, divided

1 grilled omelette (*tamagoyaki*), 10-cm x 4-cm (page 20)

2 pickled gourd strips (*kanpyo*), each 10-cm x 3-cm

4 circles of seaweed for eyes

4 circles of ham for cheeks

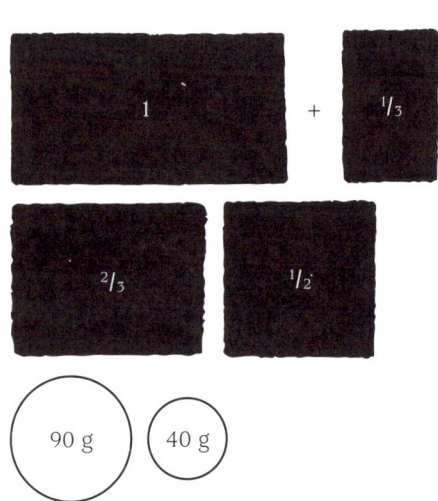

1. Cut the grilled omelette lengthwise into 3 parts for the body.

2. Trim the pickled gourd strips to the size of the grilled omelette. Place a strip between each piece of omelette.

3. Wrap the grilled omelette with $2/3$ sheet of seaweed. Set aside.

4. Shape 30 g white rice into a 10-cm oblong on $1/2$ sheet of seaweed. Roll up.

5. Cut the oblong lengthwise in half for the wings. Set aside.

6. Spread 90 g white rice on the $1\,1/3$ sheet of seaweed, leaving a 6-cm gap at one end.

7. Place the wrapped grilled omelette in the centre, followed by the wings, cut-side down.

8. Use the remaining white rice to fill any gaps before closing the roll.

9. Slice the roll into 4 pieces. Finish with a seaweed eye and ham cheek.

Sakura Flower

Ingredients

$^2/_3$ sheet of seaweed

1 strip of seaweed,
10-cm x $1^1/_2$-cm

45 g pink sushi rice
(Mix evenly: 35 g white
sushi rice + 10 g pink fish
flakes (*oboro*))

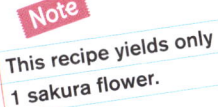

Note

This recipe yields only
1 sakura flower.

$^2/_3$

1. Spread 45 g of pink rice on $^2/_3$ sheet of seaweed, leaving a 2-cm gap at one end.

2. Place a strip of seaweed on the edge of the rice.

3. Fold the roll up tightly.

4. Press on one side to form a teardrop-shaped roll.

5. Use a chopstick to press down on the wider end of the roll to create a ridge.

6. Slice the roll into 5 pieces and arrange in the shape of a flower.

Chestnut

~ Ingredients ~

1 sheet + $^1/_3$ sheet of seaweed, joined

1 x $^2/_3$ sheet of seaweed

1 x $^1/_2$ sheet of seaweed

120 g white sushi rice, divided

70 g dark brown sushi rice (Mix evenly: 60 g white sushi rice + 10 g bonito flakes soft rice topping (*okaka* soft *furikake*))

45 g brown sushi rice (Mix evenly: 40 g white sushi rice + 5 g roasted sesame and teriyaki sauce)

Roasted white sesame seeds

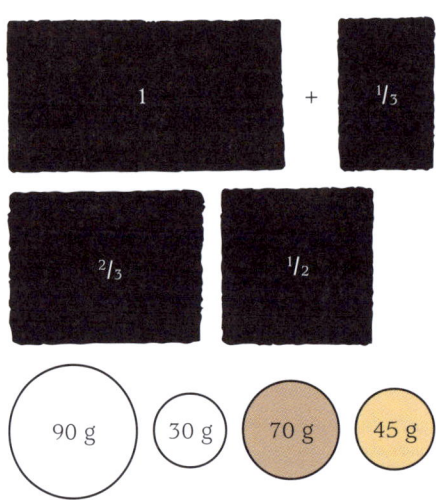

1. Shape 45 g brown rice into a 10-cm oval and wrap with $^1/_2$ sheet of seaweed.

2. Using the sushi mat, shape it into an oval for the base of the chestnut.

3. Shape 70 g dark brown rice into a 10-cm mountain for the top of the chestnut.

4. Place the wrapped oval from step 2 on a $^2/_3$ sheet of seaweed, then place the mountain from step 3 on it.

5. Close the roll up and shape to resemble a chestnut.

6. Spread 90 g white rice on the $1^1/_3$ sheet of seaweed, leaving a 6-cm gap at one end.

7. Place the chestnut roll in the centre. Sprinkle sesame seeds on the rice.

8. Start rolling up the roll. Use the remaining white rice to fill any gaps before closing the roll.

9. Slice the roll into 4 pieces.

3

4

5

7

Watermelon

Ingredients

1 sheet + $^1/_2$ sheet of seaweed, joined

2 x $^1/_2$ sheet of seaweed

30 g white sushi rice

50 g green sushi rice (Mix evenly: 40 g white sushi rice + 10 g chopped marinated seaweed (*chuka wakame*))

120 g red sushi rice (Mix evenly: 100 g white sushi rice + 20 g pink fish flakes (*oboro*)), divided

2 pickled gourd strips (*kanpyo*), 10-cm x 2-cm, each cut lengthwise into 3 strips

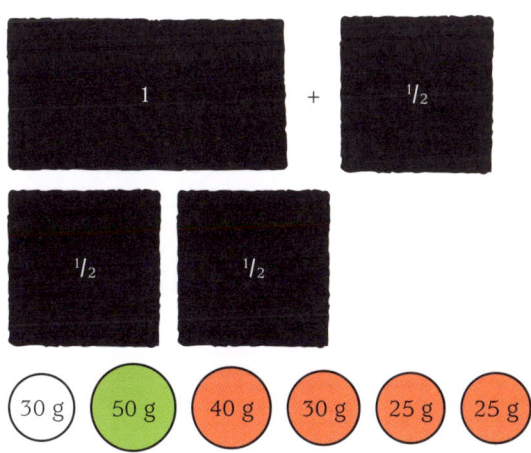

1. Spread 50 g green rice in the centre of the 1 1/2 sheet of seaweed, shaping it 6-cm wide for the rind.

2. Place 1/2 sheet of seaweed over the green rice and fold down the sides.

3. Spread with 30 g white rice, shaping it 5-cm wide for the white flesh. Cover with 1/2 sheet of seaweed.

4. Repeat to spread 40 g red rice on the seaweed, shaping it 4-cm wide for the red flesh.

5. Use a skewer to make 3 indents, then place a pickled gourd strip into each indent for the seeds.

6. Top with 30 g red rice, then make 2 indents for another 2 pickled gourd strips.

7. Top with 25 g red rice, followed by the last pickled gourd strip.

8. Cover with 25 g red rice, shaping it with a pointed top to resemble a wedge of watermelon.

9. Close up the roll.

10. Slice the roll into 4 triangular pieces.

Lemon

Ingredients

1 sheet + $^1/_3$ sheet of seaweed, joined

3 x $^1/_2$ sheet of seaweed

1 x $^2/_3$ sheet of seaweed

125 g white sushi rice, divided

90 g yellow sushi rice (Mix evenly: 75 g white sushi rice + 1 hard-boiled egg yolk), divided into 3 parts, each 30 g

1 large egg sheet (thin grilled omelette)

Roasted white sesame seeds

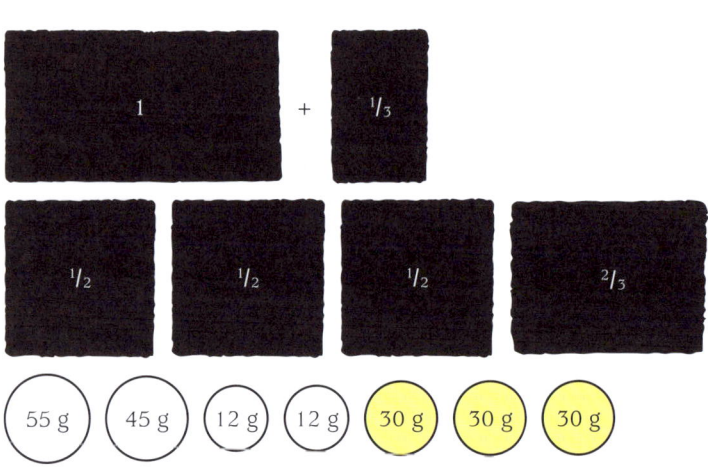

1. Shape each portion of yellow rice into an equilateral triangle with 2-cm sides. Make each 10-cm long.

2. Wrap each yellow rice triangle with $^1/_2$ sheet of seaweed. Set aside.

3. Shape 12 g white rice into a 10-cm x 2-cm strip. Repeat to make another strip. Set aside.

4. Alternate the yellow rice triangles with the white rice strips, packing them closely together. Set aside.

5. Spread 45 g white rice in the centre of the $1^1/_3$ sheet of seaweed, shaping it 6-cm wide.

6. Place the roll from step 4 on the rice.

7. Spread 55 g white rice thinly over the roll.

8. Place $^2/_3$ sheet of seaweed over the white rice and fold down the sides.

9. Place the egg sheet over the seaweed. Trim the edges if necessary.

10. Roll up the roll. Seal the seaweed with a few grains of sushi rice if needed.

11. Slice the roll into 4 pieces. Finish with roasted white sesame seeds for the seeds of the lemon.

Candy

Ingredients

1 sheet + $^1/_3$ sheet of seaweed, joined

2 x $^1/_2$ sheet of seaweed

4 x $^1/_4$ sheet of seaweed

80 g white sushi rice, divided into 4 parts, each 20 g

140 g purple sushi rice (Mix evenly: 140 g white sushi rice + 2 g dehydrated purple sweet potato powder), divided into 7 parts, each 20 g

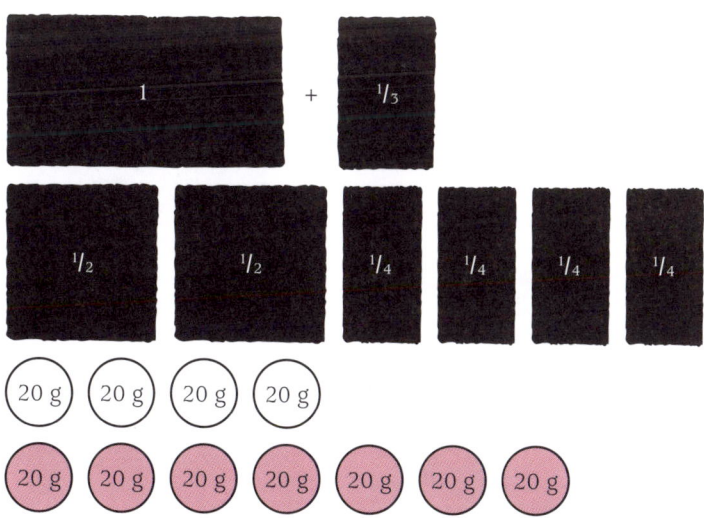

1. Spread 3 purple and 2 white parts of rice on the $1^{1}/_{3}$ sheet of seaweed. Shape each 3.5-cm wide, leaving a 3-cm gap at the end.

2. Roll the sushi up to create a spiral pattern. Slice into 4 pieces. Set aside.

3. Shape remaining portions of rice into 10-cm mountains for the sweet wrapper.

4. Arrange 2 purple and 1 white mountain on $^{1}/_{2}$ sheet of seaweed.

5. Fold two $^{1}/_{4}$ sheets of seaweed and place them in the valley between the mountains.

6. Trim the excess seaweed with a pair of scissors.

7. Repeat steps 4–6 to make another set. Slice each set into 4 pieces.

8. Assemble the parts to complete the candy.

Chick

1 sheet of seaweed

2 x $^1/_3$ sheet of seaweed

1 x $^1/_4$ sheet of seaweed

170 g yellow sushi rice
(Mix evenly: 150 g white
sushi rice + 2 hard-boiled
egg yolks), divided

1 pickled burdock
(*yamagobo*), 10-cm long

2 pickled gourd strips
(*kanpyo*), each 10-cm x
2-cm

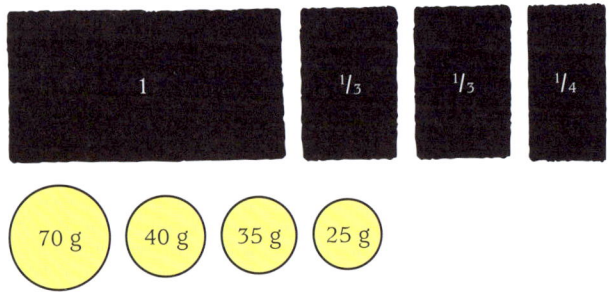

Method

1. Pat dry burdock and wrap tightly with $^1/_4$ sheet seaweed for the beak. Set aside.

2. Pat dry pickled gourd strips and wrap separately with $^1/_3$ sheet of seaweed. Roll each one up tightly for the eyes. Set aside.

3. Spread 70 g yellow rice on 1 sheet of seaweed, leaving a 4-cm gap at each end.

4. Shape 25 g yellow rice into a 10-cm long mound and place in the centre.

5. Position a rolled-up pickled gourd strip on each side of the mound for the eyes.

6. Place the rolled up burdock on top of the mound for the beak.

7. Top with 40 g yellow rice to hold the beak and eyes in place. Shape it into a dome.

8. Start rolling up the roll. Use the remaining yellow rice to fill any gaps before closing the roll.

9. Slice the roll into 4 pieces. Finish with a heart shape bento pick for the comb.

Sailing Boat

Ingredients

1 sheet + $^1/_3$ sheet of seaweed, joined

1 x $^2/_3$ sheet seaweed

1 x $^1/_2$ sheet of seaweed

1 x $^1/_3$ sheet of seaweed

160 g light green sushi rice (Mix evenly: 135 g white sushi rice + 25 g marinated seaweed (*chuka wakame*)), divided

1 mini grilled omelette (*tamagoyaki*), 10-cm x 3.5-cm (page 20)

1 Japanese fish roll (*kamaboko*), 10-cm long

1 pickled gourd strip (*kanpyo*), 10-cm x 3-cm

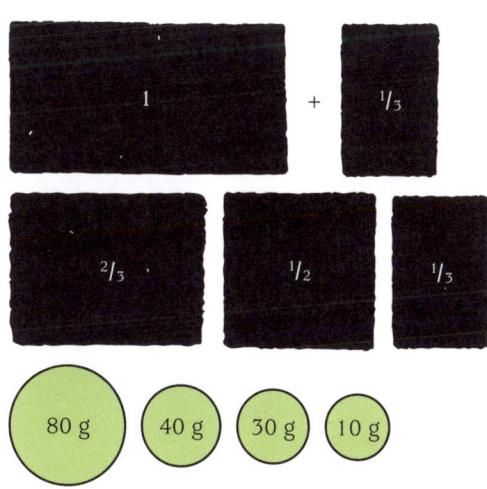

1. Trim the grilled omelette to form the hull of the sailing boat.

2. Wrap the grilled omelette with $^2/_3$ sheet of seaweed. Set aside.

3. Cut the fish roll in half for the sail. Set the other half aside for use in another recipe.

4. Wrap the fish roll with $^1/_2$ sheet of seaweed. Set aside.

5. Pat dry the pickled gourd strip and wrap with $^1/_3$ sheet of seaweed for the mast. Set aside.

6. Spread 80 g green rice on the $1\,^1/_3$ sheet of seaweed, leaving a 5-cm gap at each end.

7. Place the wrapped grilled omelette in the centre.

8. Spread 10 g green rice on one side of the grilled omelette.

9. Place the wrapped fish roll on the rice and the wrapped pickled gourd strip on the flat-side of the fish roll.

10. Spread 40 g green rice on the wrapped pickled gourd strip to fill the gap.

11. Start rolling up the roll. Use the remaining green rice to fill any gaps before closing the roll.

12. Slice the roll into 4 pieces.

Heart

~~~~~ Ingredients ~~~~~

1 sheet + $^1/_3$ sheet of seaweed, joined

1 x $^2/_3$ sheet of seaweed

1 x $^1/_8$ sheet of seaweed

125 g white sushi rice, divided

100 g pink sushi rice (Mix evenly: 85 g white sushi rice + 15 g pink fish floss (*sakura denbu*))

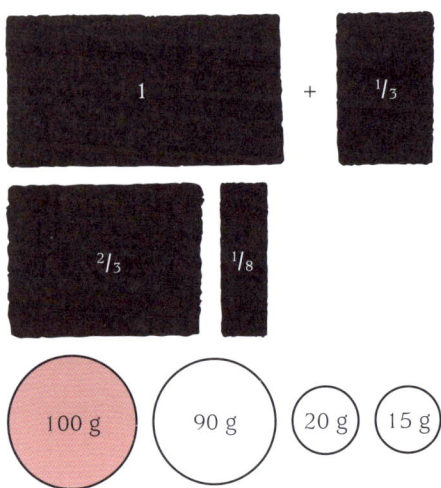

1. Shape 100 g pink rice into a 10-cm long cylinder.

2. Wrap with $^2/_3$ sheet of seaweed and use the sushi mat to shape the roll triangularly.

3. Make a shallow cut on one side of the roll using a knife.

4. Fold the $^1/_8$ sheet of seaweed lengthwise in half and place it into the cut to define the heart shape.

5. Fill the gap with 15 g white rice.

6. Spread 90 g white rice on the $1\,^1/_3$ sheet of seaweed, leaving a 5-cm gap at each end.

7. Place the heart shape roll on the rice, cut-side down.

8. Start rolling up the roll. Use the remaining white rice to fill any gaps before closing the roll.

9. Slice the roll into 4 pieces.

3

4

5

7

Quantities for this book are given in Metric and American (spoon and cup) measures. Standard spoon and cup measurements used are: 1 teaspoon = 5 ml, 1 tablespoon = 15 ml and 1 cup = 250 ml. All measures are level unless otherwise stated.

LIQUID AND VOLUME MEASURES

Metric	Imperial	American
5 ml	$1/6$ fl oz	1 teaspoon
10 ml	$1/3$ fl oz	1 dessertspoon
15 ml	$1/2$ fl oz	1 tablespoon
60 ml	2 fl oz	$1/4$ cup (4 tablespoons)
85 ml	$2^1/2$ fl oz	$1/3$ cup
90 ml	3 fl oz	$3/8$ cup (6 tablespoons)
125 ml	4 fl oz	$1/2$ cup
180 ml	6 fl oz	$3/4$ cup
250 ml	8 fl oz	1 cup
300 ml	10 fl oz ($1/2$ pint)	$1^1/4$ cups
375 ml	12 fl oz	$1^1/2$ cups
435 ml	14 fl oz	$1^3/4$ cups
500 ml	16 fl oz	2 cups
625 ml	20 fl oz (1 pint)	$2^1/2$ cups
750 ml	24 fl oz ($1^1/5$ pints)	3 cups
1 litre	32 fl oz ($1^3/5$ pints)	4 cups
1.25 litres	40 fl oz (2 pints)	5 cups
1.5 litres	48 fl oz ($2^2/5$ pints)	6 cups
2.5 litres	80 fl oz (4 pints)	10 cups

DRY MEASURES

Metric	Imperial
30 grams	1 ounce
45 grams	1$^{1}/_{2}$ ounces
55 grams	2 ounces
70 grams	2$^{1}/_{2}$ ounces
85 grams	3 ounces
100 grams	3$^{1}/_{2}$ ounces
110 grams	4 ounces
125 grams	4$^{1}/_{2}$ ounces
140 grams	5 ounces
280 grams	10 ounces
450 grams	16 ounces (1 pound)
500 grams	1 pound, 1$^{1}/_{2}$ ounces
700 grams	1$^{1}/_{2}$ pounds
800 grams	1$^{3}/_{4}$ pounds
1 kilogram	2 pounds, 3 ounces
1.5 kilograms	3 pounds, 4$^{1}/_{2}$ ounces
2 kilograms	4 pounds, 6 ounces

LENGTH

Metric	Imperial
0.5 cm	$^{1}/_{4}$ inch
1 cm	$^{1}/_{2}$ inch
1.5 cm	$^{3}/_{4}$ inch
2.5 cm	1 inch

ABBREVIATION

tsp	teaspoon
Tbsp	tablespoon
g	gram
kg	kilogram
ml	millilitre

The recipes in this book were taken from *Kawaii Deco Sushi*, first published in 2015.

Photographer: Calvin Tan

Published by Marshall Cavendish Cuisine
An imprint of Marshall Cavendish International

A member of the
Times Publishing Group

Other Marshall Cavendish Offices:
Marshall Cavendish Corporation. 99 White Plains Road, Tarrytown NY 10591-9001, USA • Marshall Cavendish International (Thailand) Co Ltd. 253 Asoke, 12th Flr, Sukhumvit 21 Road, Klongtoey Nua, Wattana, Bangkok 10110, Thailand • Marshall Cavendish (Malaysia) Sdn Bhd, Times Subang, Lot 46, Subang Hi-Tech Industrial Park, Batu Tiga, 40000 Shah Alam, Selangor Darul Ehsan, Malaysia

Marshall Cavendish is a registered trademark of Times Publishing Limited

National Library Board, Singapore Cataloguing-in-Publication Data

Names: Wong, Shirley (Writer on bento cooking). | Tan, Calvin, photographer.
Title: Get started making fun sushi / Little Miss Bento, Shirley Wong ; photographer Calvin Tan.
Other title(s): Get started making
Description: Singapore : Marshall Cavendish Cuisine, [2017]
Identifiers: OCN 1003327046 | 978-981-47-9414-5 (hardcover)
Subjects: LCSH: Cooking, Japanese. | Sushi. | LCGFT: Cookbooks.
Classification: DDC 641.5952--dc23

Printed by Times Offset (M) Sdn Bhd